*Operation Memory*

PRINCETON SERIES OF CONTEMPORARY POETS

For other books in the series, see page 87.

Operation Memory

BY DAVID LEHMAN

PRINCETON UNIVERSITY PRESS, PRINCETON, NEW JERSEY

Copyright © 1990 by David Lehman
Published by Princeton University Press, 41 William Street,
Princeton, New Jersey 08540
In the United Kingdom: Princeton University Press, Oxford

Library of Congress Cataloging-in-Publication Data

Lehman, David, 1948-
Operation memory / David Lehman.
p.   cm.—(Princeton series of contemporary poets)
ISBN 0-691-06848-8 (alk. paper)
ISBN 0-691-01482-5 (pbk. : alk. paper)
I. Title. II. Series.
PS3562.E428O64   1990
811'.54—dc20   89-29072

Publication of this book has been aided by a grant
from the Lacy Lockert Fund of Princeton University Press
This book has been composed in Linotron Trump Medieval

Princeton University Press books are printed on acid-free paper,
and meet the guidelines for permanence and durability of the
Committee on Production Guidelines for Book Longevity of the
Council on Library Resources

Printed in the United States of America by Princeton University Press,
Princeton, New Jersey

10 9 8 7 6 5 4 3 2 1
10 9 8 7 6 5 4 3 2 1
(Pbk.)

FOR STEFANIE

Contents

Part Four

Acknowledgments

Grateful acknowledgment is made to the magazines in which these poems first appeared:

Boulevard: "The American Religion"; "Museum, 1980"; "New York City, 1974"

The Gettysburg Review: "Pascal's Wager"

Michigan Quarterly Review: "For I Will Consider Your Dog Molly"

New American Writing: "Arrival at Kennedy"; "Heaven"

The New Republic: "Rejection Slip"; "The Survivors," part 3 (as "Our Hero")

The New York Review of Books: "With Tenure"; "One Size Fits All: A Critical Essay"

Ontario Review: "The Square Root of Minus One"

The Paris Review: "Four Versions of the End"; "Henry James: The Movie"; "Mythologies"; "Perfidia"

Partisan Review: "The Desire for Strange Cities"; "Gallery Notes"

Poetry New York: "Vietnam Memorial"

Scripsi (Australia): "Defective Story"; "The Delayed Reaction"; "The Right Number"

Shenandoah: "Fear"; "Operation Memory"; "Plato's Retreat"; "Spontaneous Combustion"; "Spontaneous Generation"

The Yale Review: "The Answering Stranger"; "Cambridge, 1972"

"The Survivors," part 2, appeared in my essay "In the Holocaust Gallery" in *Testimony*, ed. David Rosenberg, published in 1989 by Times Books, a division of Random House, Inc. "The Desire for Strange Cities" appeared as a Nimbus Broadside in 1987. My thanks to the editors and publishers concerned. I also want to thank the National Endowment for the Arts and the John Simon Guggenheim Memorial Foundation for grants that helped support the writing of this book.

—D.L.

Part One

1.

Thanks to the truth serum, no one forgot
The exact spot where each of us was standing
Waiting for an accusation, an explanation, or a miracle
Like suspects gathered in a gloomy drawing room
When the phone rang, as we knew it would,
And Uncle Joe gave his orders with his customary brevity
Forbidding us to answer the door. There was a knock.

The condemned man waited while we deliberated
Behind closed doors. The thermometer said zero
Though the truth serum made it July 1934.
He stood at the door, shivering in the cold,
With the patience of a child who lives in parables
And knows he will never enter the house.
There was a knock. We thought it was the police.

There was a knock. But no one was there when we looked.
Back on the phone, my sister Joan tried to sound reasonable.
All we had to do was answer a riddle: name the caller
Who visits you only when no one is home. "The fate
Of an innocent man depends on your reply," said Uncle Joe.
"There's no need for him to die." Could we
Have saved him with a lie? In any case, we didn't.

2.

Suddenly it was as though observation were action,
The one form of action that fatalism allowed
Since it left one's innocence intact or
Cloaked it in skepticism: and we who had always meant
To believe in the will stood helplessly by

3

Like relatives of the deceased, listening to lawyers deny
Our right to contest the old man's testament.

So it was decided: history had already happened,
And all we could do was watch a batch of old film clips
Chronicling the catastrophe: armistice signings
In railway cars, barbed wire borders,
The stunned faces of the American soldiers
And the grinning skeletons that greeted them where
They had dug their own graves: and here

Was one who had escaped in the night
And crawled and then walked and then ran in the night
Until he reached a nearby farm and knocked on the door
And stood there, wondering whether he'd be saved,
When a shrill voice from behind the shut door
Uttered its unequivocal reply: Jew, go back to your grave.
It was, thanks to the truth serum, July 1944.

3.

The corpse on the operating table shakes itself back to life.
"We knew we had three wishes only
And had to save up the third
In case we goofed with the other two
And needed to become children again."
Our hero refuses to understand, though prodded by
A blind man with a revolver in his hand.

Our hero, who wasn't always a hero, lives
In despair, but pretends not to care.
He disagrees with reality. That is his right,
And he has scars to prove it. Switch off the light
And he will follow the slowest most voluptuous curve
Between any two stars, elaborating the distance
Before spanning it in a leap of forgetfulness.

The note he left in invisible ink was held to the light
Two days too late. Yet he survives the cause of his distress,
Lifts his former bride, still in her wedding dress,
And declares the weight, by a miracle of logic,
To agree with the dictionary definition of time.
Merely to have carried it was a moral action,
However futile, whatever the merits of the fiction.

All at once it hits you: the hand comes down
Hard, like a wall, smashing the wall
That was there, dividing the air. Look closely.
Forget about the lines on the open palm,
The numbers tattooed on the hero's outstretched arm.
It wouldn't be a jail cell if it didn't have
A ladder in one corner and a patient asleep in bed.

The other heroes died in their sleep, or ours,
But were immortal nevertheless: they had to be:
Otherwise we'd never have believed in them to begin with.
Begin with a Molotov cocktail party
At a posh Manhattan brownstone. The fun has just begun.
It wouldn't be a hospital room if it didn't have
A window too high for the survivor to see through.

As the wrong man falls down the elevator shaft,
Relaxing his muscles to soften the blow,
Forget about the numbers, and what they meant,
The door, and why it was always shut,
The three drops of blood on the snow.
It wouldn't be a cave if it didn't have
Shadows on the wall, dancing in the dark, in silence.

The boy hid under the house
With his dog, his red lunch box, and his fear
Thinking God is near
Thinking It's time to leave the things that mean
Just one thing, though you can't tell what that is,
Like God or death. The boy held his breath,
Closed his eyes, and disappeared,
Thinking No one will find me here—

But only when his parents were watching.
When they weren't, he slipped away
And hid under the house
And stayed there all night, and through the next day,
Until Father (who had died that December)
Agreed to come home, and Mother was twenty
Years younger again, and pregnant with her
Darling son. Hiding under the house,
He could see it all, past and future,
The deep blue past, the black and white future,
Until he closed his eyes and made it disappear,

And everyone was glad when he returned
To the dinner table, a grown man
With wire-rim glasses and neatly combed hair.
Fear was the name of his dog, a German shepherd.

The title doesn't have to have
    anything to do with what
Is depicted: "Dance You Monster
    to My Soft Song,"
"The King and Queen Surrounded by
    Swift Nudes."
We see what we want to see when
    we aren't looking.
Elegant angels in dinner jackets dance
    with nudes wearing
Red slippers, and clouds sail in
    through open windows.
Process is everything—the process
    of assimilation
(A freshly made bed with giant-sized
    toiletries on it),
The process of elimination (the bather
    emerges on the shore,
His forehead a blank). These are
    the instructions and these
The warnings you will hear: eliminate
    the model and she
Will have her revenge; eliminate the sky
    but save the stars;
Enlarge the rose to fill the canvas;
    eliminate yellow.
Then put it all back in and see what
    happens. Eliminate the model:
Look at her look at herself in the mirror
    before it cracks
Into a cobwebbed windshield, and the car
    radio's still playing

As the children walk away from the wreck.
     Suddenly the viewer
Is going to die, and knows it. The thought
     occurs to him at least
Once a day. Then come the boyhood flashes
     and the fear of having left
Something undone, but never knowing what.
     "This is the world I want
To live in: a place where the man who thinks
     he has no illusions has
At least that one; where his speechless son
     can fill his mouth
With pebbles, and learn to outshout the sea."

Defective Story

The doctors know what can be done
For the man in the mirror who hazards all he has:
Faced with a choice of three caskets,
He chooses the one made out of lead,
Wakes up dazed in the recovery room
With a black eye and a sheet over his head,
Floats out of bed, and proceeds
To trace on the rim of his useless hat
A halo of snow he knows he must shed
If, like a ship without a rudder, he would sail,
With angst his guide, exposed to wind and hail.

Who you are, who you think you are,
Wears a patch over the left eye and a forehead scar
That makes all the girls want to sleep with him.
Day breaks like a bloodshot eye. All roads lead
To the place where three roads meet, and what
Awaits us there is an old-fashioned detective story
Pretending to be a metaphysical riddle. Thus,
The real clues smell like red herrings to us
And, grateful for her grace, death leaves
His calling card in the lame sister's hand
Whom to embrace would obtain for the suitor
What many men desire, and later renounce.

The successful lovers stayed in seasonal hotel rooms
With signs behind the doors saying, "In case of fire,
Do not shout fire. Gardez votre sang-froid!"
Sometimes Anna felt faint, especially in crowds,
Though an afternoon nap proved an apt antidote
To battle fatigue. The body in action, stripped
Of guilt, tripped the light fantastic. Clouds
Lined the umbrella that sheltered the tiny boat.

Yes doesn't come without a struggle.
No is the square root of yes.
Before there was yes there was no,
As if speech meant denial, an infant reflex,
The feeble exercise of the will when
It was locked in a body too puny for it.
And before the first no, there was hunger.

All that is easy enough to understand,
Now that they are children, able to speak and think
And understand as children, relying on faith
To lead them out of the forest where they met
A dwarf wearing the mask of a man with a broken nose.
They know that *evil* spells *live* backwards;
They believe in spells and trances and signs
And are sure to betray the wild creatures that befriend them.
Yet their innocence survives. Watch them sleep
And wake, as the light bisects the forest
And points them home, where they've never been.

And yes, I, too, have great plans for them
And can almost see them turn back before
Their shadows carry them across the border
And on, into the land of nothingness. But, of course,
It already is too late, and has been all along,
Ever since we first heard them cry out in hunger.
Will they collect their tears in silver bowls
For the ritual washing of hands? Are they likely
To link their numberless arms
Like atoms with an orbiting electron in common?
No, I can't see how it can be done.

But, then, the square root of minus one
Mystifies me, for all the tutelage I've received:

It's as though I were alive in Austria
At the turn of the century, a schoolboy in a military academy
Who believes in a god of reason rather than
A god of temper-tantrums, needing constant placating.
An admirable skeptic in a starched school uniform,
The boy can't, or won't, suspend his disbelief
Perhaps because his belief won't survive
So harmless a test as this: that we can conceive
Of numbers for things that don't exist, assign them values,
And construct vast mathematical edifices around them,
Monuments to absence and negation. Credit the notion
And we're back at square one, only
The rules have changed in the middle of the game.

So it's understandable if, knowing that we should know better,
We refuse to admit the obvious truth
About these demons in pine forests, these weird sisters
And brothers grim, all of whom are real, as angels are real
And threatening. All our evasions are understandable:
It's possible, after all, to comprehend a fact
While shying away from its consequences, and what matter if this
Reduces history itself to the level of a fairy tale, a pattern
Of episodes between one syntactical formula and another?
If it's possible to believe things without believing *in* anything,
The reverse is equally true. Affirmation depends on denial,
Yes on no, and sometimes the imagination must balk:
Just as I can't quite bring myself to square
The image of a circular fire, circumference extended
Beyond all known limits of space and duration
Whose center was mortal terror
And whose casualties add up to one nation
Invisible, negated, in death serene, and indivisible
From the horizon, where sea and sky meet, and vanish.

Once you lose it, it keeps coming back to you, forever.
A seductive notion: "now" is the price of eternal "then,"
A religious corollary to the theme of beauty and "easeful death."
And I suppose that's what we mean when we say
"This is what heaven must be like," or else heaven is the sum
Of all the comparisons that poets, writing with a gun
To their heads, propose in the terror of the moment.
But to recover the loss before suffering its absence,
To lose it on a yesterday that never was and have it back
On the endless plateau of today, is really what I had in mind,
That and the knowledge that something forgotten always has
A delayed echo, like an echo frozen on northern seas
To be released with the voices of winter mariners
In the summer thaw. In a dream, I forgot to write down
The words of the dream, and who had spoken them to me,
And what we were doing in this rented car we were driving
Across Los Angeles, from one end to the other, though
We knew this to be a physical impossibility: the end
Is what we cannot reach, or want to, Los Angeles being
One example. I turned to you in the car and said
I wanted to write a play called "The End of the World
In L.A." Somehow I knew that the world would end there
If an ending were possible. "If you're wrong," you said,
"It's a one-minute mistake." You didn't say what you meant,
Or you did, but I forgot to write down the words. In a dream,
I heard shots at ten-minute intervals. I turned to you
In bed but you weren't there: you were in Los Angeles,
Driving with me toward the end of the world
And the Pacific Ocean. In the infinite distance between
Here and there, the arrow paused without ceasing to move
Toward the moving target to the west of the horizon.
Only a second had gone by. And I knew I had you back, forever.

Reduce the supply while the demand stays constant and the
    result is
No taxis for anybody. Reddening sky, the threat of rain, my
    cabbie's demented laugh
As he lights up a joint & news of Jackie Gleason's death
    comes on the radio.
This is my city, I know that now, though I recognize hardly
    any of the streets.
I'm three drinks ahead of the rest of the cast & trying hard
    to keep my eyes
On Eurydice in the rear-view mirror, who tells me I've arrived,
    welcomes me home,
And warns me to focus on the road ahead. I'd rather have my
    arms around you,
Dear, in the backseat of heaven. Meanwhile, a siren goes off
    in front of the old
Neighborhood hardware store, where a sailor and his girl kissed
    under the awning
And became our parents during World War II. We pass them in
    the cab & feel
Nostalgic for the city before we were born: big band music,
    Rita Hayworth,
Gray fedoras, and the Third Avenue El. In the end, of course,
    we forget why we came,
What brought us together in the lovely humid August night we
    thought would never end
When freedom meant driving a car over a cliff & jumping out
    at the last possible moment.

Four Versions of the End

1.

The stars have gone north, abandoning the city
For this wilderness that is mine, if only for a time,
Long enough to learn the language of the leaves before
It's time to return, like an unwilling prophet,
To warn the others of the danger they face
And there's nothing they can do about it, except listen.

2.

Is it enough to have survived the crash,
To escape the burning car and run,
With the confidence of a sleepwalker, along
The border between two foreign states of mind
And not look back, lest we freeze into statues
Of ourselves, awed by the devastation behind us?

3.

Some regard the castle as a crossword puzzle of bricks,
But the forest beckons, babbling the language of brooks,
And there's nothing we can do about it, except listen
And wait, until it's too late, until
The world is everything that is the fall:
All roads lead to the same supreme heartbreak.

4.

On the abandoned airfield you can almost hear
The silence getting louder, coming nearer,

Speeding by and then, with a whine like the smear
Of a siren, diminishing in pitch as it fades
Into one man's past, which is another man's future,
And there's nothing you can do about it, except listen.

The Right Number

FOR RON HORNING

"I'll be a man for you," sang the voice on the radio.
And you, the listener in your living room, know
You are avoiding your destiny (and confirming it:
Yours is the destiny of the man who wanted to avoid it).
The phone doesn't ring, but if it did
It would be a summons from headquarters in New York.
It would be the voice of an unmarried woman.

You are immediately put on hold. The muzak begins
In your right ear: "I'll be a fool for you."
It could be the voice of a woman you used to sleep with.
To while away the minutes you free-associate
On a doodle pad but draw a blank on the word Jew.
You see a trio of owls flying in a winter landscape
Rather than a man and woman in bed. Is that significant?
An unfamiliar voice pipes up: "You've called the right number."

It sounds like a prerecorded message but you're glad to have it
Anyway: "The road of mirth leads to the palace of anger.
He who leaps cheerfully into the void
Owes no explanations to anyone." You write it down
On the doodle pad, vowing to be better prepared
The next time you are put on hold. You replace
The receiver. When you look out the window you see
What was there twenty-four hours ago. Nobody else does.

The Eros Construction Company has taken over the project.
You see their trucks everywhere, their cranes,
Their wrecking balls. What else are these bridges and towers
But monuments to Eros, "builder of cities"? Yet not all
Is well. Something is missing, and it's the reason you came
To this bridge connecting land and fog, the old city and the new:

17

"On this bridge, spies in novels carried umbrellas and wore
Bowler hats," says a man's voice in accents weary and nostalgic.
"On that side of the river stands the clocktower,
And what it stands for: procreation, comfort, family life.
On this side is the mystery and melancholy of a street,
Which you will discover as you race
Like a girl to the tip of the giant's shadow,
Where she disappears, owing no explanations to anyone."

The Answering Stranger

1.

Here is your childhood: a boy running.
I have cold hands. Mother, may I stay at home today?
On the radio the Japanese are bombing Pearl Harbor
In the middle of a football game. The phone rings.
"You either live too long or die too young,"
The caller says. "That's why you need insurance."

You either live too long or die too young—
Nothing else is real, not even your childhood.
Here is your childhood: a man running,
A boy running down the rungs of the fire escape,
A man driving his car through a stop sign,
An ambulance siren, your first naked body.

2.

Father forgives his enemies, but first he sees them hanged.
Mother is waiting for the knock on the door. Nobody
Is the stranger on the other side of the door
But nobody is the wiser: a single lie explodes
The testimony given under duress by one

Who saw it all, was there, and suffered
The heightened sensitivity of a bug, strutting up and down
The keyboard. "Everything I do
Is an experiment," he thinks. And therefore
He throws people off trains, or blows them up in Arabia.

3.

The anesthesia did wonders for Father's memory.
It seems that everyone in the audience is talking about him,

Though he doesn't exist. A single lie explodes
The rose, which expands to fill the entire room.
I heard the footsteps. You can't tell me the house is empty.
The caller says, "That's why you need insurance."

The big blonde in the dormitory blames her bad orgasms on Daddy.
The bearded bully puts the blame on Mame.
I am writing this not for you but for them,
The invisible others, waiting for the phone to stop ringing.
The boy who saved you from drowning says,
"Here is your childhood: cigarettes in puddles."

4.

The impotent colonel ordered the false confession.
A bugging device had been planted in the chandelier.
"Please extinguish all smoking materials," the role model says.
She welcomes you to the twentieth century.

The Twentieth Century is the name of a train that no longer runs.
The bomb in the briefcase goes off, but the tyrant survives
And the train no longer runs. I heard the footsteps.
I saw the footprints. But the path led only one way.

The captain turns on the landing lights.
A fire has broken out in the cabin.
Yet I keep waiting for the knock on the door.
Nothing else is real, not even the ashes.

Everywhere I go I can smell the fear.
Nothing else is real, not even the ashes
Of the boy who saved you from drowning
Or the stranger on the other side of the door.

Listen closely or you won't hear, though
A bugging device has been planted in the chandelier,
Which expands to fill the entire room.
Here is your childhood: a boy running.

"Please extinguish all smoking materials," the role model says.
I am writing this not for you but for her,
The naked girl dancing on the roof, who welcomes you
To the twentieth century, though she doesn't exist.

Part Two

Mythologies

I.

The question is not how like the animals we are
But how we got that way. We laugh, for what is a suicide note

But the epitaph of an emotion? Few of us die out in the open;
And when you say thesis, I say antithesis,

But we don't stop there: we take our opposing ideas,
Plant them on opposing cliffs and then build a footbridge

Between them, seemingly flimsy yet sturdy enough in fact
To support a battalion. Hidden behind trees, we watch

The soldiers march across it, single file, too scared
To look down. We cheer them all, all except the boy

In the fairy tale who knew no fear. Him we pity.
He laughs open-eyed, ready to die as we were not.

He is one of us, all right, but better, stronger, stranger.
He asks for more fear than anyone can bear.

II.

The guilty had three choices: awkward chords of candor,
Canned laughter, or the wild hyacinth's sutra, before

Silence returned triumphant, and the journey resumed
In darkness, though the sky above was classically blue.

Everyone kept his opinion to himself
As harmony dictated, and effigies of Tristan and Isolde

Accompanied their stubborn footsteps across the wild
Terrain. Yet the longing for a loud catharsis

At night renewed their pain. "If only we could climb
Out of these clouds and heartfelt headaches,

Like ravished children in the glory of a snowball fight
After school, and never again have to descend,

Who would not abandon these erotic shipwrecks
And fall asleep like tigers in the destined heights?"

III.

At a festival of conceptual art in Cairo,
I saw a tank buried entirely in snow.

I knew then that silence is the source
Of all music, all laughter, all thought, and so

I stuffed pebbles in my mouth and stood by the sea
And roared my defiance of the waves. It was here,

Years before, that our plane and its shadow
Converged: I ran from the fire, carrying the flames

In my arms. I ran and ran, feeling like a man
Fighting a newspaper on a windy beach, but it wasn't

A beach at all: the sand beneath me was snow,
Is snow, and the spears in the desert sky look like stars.

In the pyramid's triangular shadow, I was the man
Who heard the crimson explosion, and ran. And ran.

IV.

Keats in one of his letters says, "My Imagination
Is a Monastery and I am its Monk." I wonder.

If a man's imagination is his monastery,
This place looks a lot like an empty railway station,

King's Cross in London or the Gare St. Lazare in Paris,
A place whose smoke and fog Monet dissolved

Into a chorus of colors. There we stood, my love and I,
Having made our vows under the suspended clock,

Hero and bride. But as we walked away, side by side,
Down the station's sunless nave, amid the excitement

Of the crowd, and foreign languages spoken loud,
We knew our exile had already begun, could hear

The conductor's shrill whistle, could see the light
At the end of the tunnel, where the battlefields begin.

V.

Paradise was hardly what Psyche
With her bleeding blackberries and nervous orgasms

Could have foretold, enjoyed,
And renounced for the sake of some querulous abstraction

Designed to keep us unhappy but alive.
Call it civilization. Call our disobedience instinctive.

Or say we obeyed an angry muse, who ordered us to dance.
"Or else?" I asked. She sighed before answering.

"Or else a dismal armchair will be your lot
With chamber music your sole narcotic—music that will make

You face your former self, and grieve over incidents
Scarcely recalled, and eat without pleasure, and drink

Without thirst, and dread what shall never come to pass."
In the revelation of our nakedness, we danced.

VI.

"A ball that is caught is fuller, by the weight
Of its return, than the same ball thrown." Our empty hands say so.

We feel free. In the other room the true believers remain,
The ones who insist that evil is real, the only real thing.

Cannibals and missionaries they are, accomplices in sin,
Greedy for punishment, to inflict or endure it.

We are glad to leave them behind, glad not to have to hear
Their chants and wails. Down the elevator we go

And out into the canyon created by skyscraper shadows.
Yet even we, dedicated as we are to good living,

Sometimes walk around with a lost look on our faces,
As if the blessing for a piece of fruit or cup of wine

Had suddenly come to mind, though cup and plate are empty;
Had come to mind and faded almost instantly away.

VII.

Admit it: you used to walk around thinking there had
To be a reason for things, for everything. That way

Paranoia lies. Not a science of syllables, the solitude
Total, but the prophet's lit lantern was what you wanted—

And what you got was "neon in daylight," a pleasure
Recommended by Frank O'Hara. Those pleasures meant a lot to you,

You even thought you lived for them, until the first death
(A nervous uncle broke the news when you landed at Kennedy)

And the first marriage (you stayed up all night and read
Beyond the Pleasure Principle, a fair description

Of your lovemaking). It seems that new myths are needed
And consumed all the time by folks like you. Each erases the last,

Producing tomorrow's tabula rasa, after a night of dreams
In which the tigers of wrath become the tigers of repose.

VIII.

Go back to the beginning, to the first fist fight.
They played for high stakes those days. The penalty for losing

Was death or slavery, take your pick. To spare a life
Was the mark of the master; the mark of his slave

Was fear. Noble savage, nothing. Forget about paradise.
My vote goes to Hobbes's "life of man, solitary, poor,

Nasty, brutish, and short." An amazing sentence:
The syllable that ends it also lends it its poignancy,

Since we go on wanting what we can scarcely bear.
Go back, go back, back to when god became a swan

With beautiful wounded wings, and raped the astonished maiden.
Back to the dream that stays real when you wake up,

Accustomed to your hunger and clinging to it,
Like a panther accustomed to his cage. Go back.

IX.

A slap in the face, and the face burns with shame.
Anger comes later, comes stranger, looking for someone to blame.

End of message. Can't see the stars;
Can't say anything that hasn't been said before

By somebody slamming the door; can only repeat
The syntax that brought the crowd to its feet

In the silence that appeased the nightingale.
End of tale. But its moral was simple:

I lost the hearing in one of my ears
And listened with the other to a deaf man's

Symphony. He built a heaven out of his fears
That there wasn't one. End of nightmare.

—The imperfect past, going by too fast,
Begged us to collect it. It couldn't last.

X.

The doctor put his cards on the table.
"Take your pick," he said. He was able

To offer me fear of extinction or fear of pain,
Though freedom from neither. "You mustn't complain."

In the vertiginous air, the monks wore masks
To keep their germs to themselves and their

Identities a secret. A hero to his own valet,
The Sultan choreographed his murderous ballet

Until Scheherazade, entering the circus tent
With John the Baptist's head on a silver tray,

Told her tale and made the crowd repent.
The curtain dropped and the crowd went on its way,

But no one could say what the nightmare meant,
Or why it was sent to us, or by whom it was sent.

XI.

You can't have it, so you want it, or
You couldn't have it, so you no longer want it, or

You're stuck with it, forever. It was designed with you in mind,
Like the locked door that swung open majestically when you

Spoke the magic words or just answered in the affirmative when
Your name was called. "Here I am, ready to meet you,

Ready to make any sacrifice," you said,
Still in bed, wrestling with an evil angel

In your sleep. You were seventeen years old then
And woke up with a limp. Desire is like that:

The girl knows what you want and cries when
She gives it to you because it was yours because

She whispered your name in your sleeping ear
And said: "Here I am." And was gone a minute later.

XII.

I met her in one of those sleazebag bars—
I think it was called The Bottom Line—in Buffalo,

Self-proclaimed "city of no illusions," where
Silent men in shirtsleeves sit on bar stools and watch

Girls with tattoos on their buttocks strip
Down to g-strings and panties. They dance to the thump

Of moronic music, grind and hump under hot strobe lights,
And then, when the act is over, circulate among the scumbags,

Gyrating in front of each in turn, making each feel special,
And each, aroused by the mingled smell of musk and sweat,

Folds a dollar and sticks it into her crotch for a tip.
She was different. When I left the bar that night I knew

She would follow, and she did, and I never looked back, never
Glanced at the rear-view mirror. All other women turned into her.

XIII.

Her name is Mary but was Miriam before that and soon
She will change it to Alice. What she offered was a shadow

The shape of Europe on the map above the bed of my youth.
Her shawl is all that remains of Europe in the downstairs closet.

It was forbidden to lift up her skirt and look, look.
Yet boys and girls danced across the bridal morning like a bridge

As the wings of the fog like white sails lingered
Across the bay. I flew, like a caterpillar with wings, into the new day.

That was the day we buried Europe. We built a dome in air
And in the icy silence of the tomb. To hang like a spider

On a subway strap seemed a suitable fate for some, but we
Lit a candle and watched it cast the shadow of a mountain

In a valley. It was the awful shadow of some unseen power,
A heaven in a wild flower. Europe, bloody Europe was gone.

XIV.

In the dream of your choice, you wake up
In the Garden of Eden, alone except for a whore with a heart,

Wearing a nurse's uniform. The serpent says:
Listen carefully. This is for your own good.

At the tone it will be eight o'clock.
Nine out of ten physicians recommend

That you surround yourself with the kind of sorrows
That can be instantly relieved by frivolous kisses,

With vegetables as lush as fruits
Ripening in your hands. When the hospital gates are opened,

Don't hesitate, run! And when you arrive at last in the land
Of the free, take your place in line with all of the others

As though nothing had happened between then and now
To make you doubt the conviction that you're blessed.

XV.

If you were a painter, you'd paint the wind
Green. It would shake the boughs of the honey locust trees.

It would chase the leaves across the continent.
It would scatter their crumbs in a twist of swirling snow.

It would be colorless and green at the same time,
The wind that aligns the pond and the cloud,

The wind that is everywhere, in constant motion,
As buoyant as Ariel and as scornful of gross Caliban,

The wind that holds up the fly ball, drives it back
Into fair territory, causes it to drift within reach

Of the right-fielder, who waves off the second baseman,
Until a last gust lifts the ball over both their heads

And it lands safely for the double that ends the game
In extra innings, costing our team the pennant.

XVI.

After the flood, refreshed, was the first time
You realized that the road to truth was the road

Of flagrant fiction. You surrounded yourself
With symbols (a mountain, a window, an ark,

A rainbow) and mythic creatures (the dove that returned
And the raven that didn't). You understood the dream

Of the old woman who interpreted the sailor's dream.
Then came the other birds, the clouds that come

When the rain is done, and the wind that signals
The discovery of dry land, a new continent,

As the report of a gun sounds the start of the race,
As the bottle broken beneath the bridegroom's foot

Begins the marriage, as church bells start the funeral
Parade and all the townspeople march in the procession.

XVII.

No longer is there freedom in confusion,
Nor forgiveness in confession,

Nor charm in the old illusion
Of moonlight, the tower, the howling dog, the escaping lovers,

Escaping into midnight in the Western hemisphere,
When the possibilities of expansion still seemed limitless

And the soul could choose among stars without number
In the vast velvet night without end.

—In the midst of other woe than ours, I went to the window
And cured the solitude of the listeners outside

Who shivered in the rain, waiting for the police to come
And ambulance sirens to sound. Drunk I was when

I went to the bathroom, looked in the mirror, and said,
"Dad, Dad, is that you?" In the terror of the night.

XVIII.

"Wherever you follow," he said, "I will lead."
Where summer met fall, she picked up a brittle orange leaf.

He wanted to lie on the grass, to lean and loaf
At his ease, but the crisis intervened: news of her unpaid loan

Prompted him to put his sandals on his head, as in the Zen koan.
Slowly he walked away. Silence followed, then the sound of a moan

In the room next door. So orange it seemed a painted moon
Shone against the indigo sky. And quickly her mood

Went from unreasonable euphoria to realistic dejection, as the wood
In the fireplace turned to ash without first yielding a flame. The wool

Of their sweaters had begun to unravel. "If the fool
Persists in his folly," someone said, "he will have food

Enough to eat, loaves and fishes galore. Worship the good,
Which is beautiful though untrue. Turn your back on gold."

XIX.

If we were painters we'd favor vibrant stripes,
Primary colors, flat surfaces, a lot of white

Remaining on the canvas. If we were composers
We'd take the music of exotic jungles with us

When we visit the vast vacant tundra. "If I were
Rich enough," vowed the philanthropist, "I'd move

To a magnolia mansion and spend my days
Translating modern literature into ancient Greek."

Great plans, distant vistas, a rearguard action
To sabotage the present—and here we've all assembled,

At the antiseptic airport, with haunted looks on our faces.
Occasional eye contact between man with tan and woman in white.

"You look like your voice," she says, breaking the silence.
The rest of us know where we're going, but we don't know when.

XX.

They've cornered the market on moral outrage. Yes, they have.
The more noise they make about it, the more nervous we get.

They're always telling us just how shallow we are.
The only convictions we have, they say, are on our drivers' licenses.

The charge is not entirely fair to us, though it has its grain of truth.
We tend to luxuriate in our indecisiveness. Not they. No one can say

They lack conviction and passion and certitude. We have our doubts,
Which make us less glamorous and give us

The haunted look we wear. But something in defense
Of our bemused spectatorship must be said: at least it spares us

The postures of those hypocrite lechers, brothers and others
Who sublimate their sexuality into opulent rhetoric and chide us

For not doing the same. They have our best interests at heart.
They may even be happier than we are. We have our doubts.

XXI.

Today's graffiti is in the sky: "More than meets the eye."
Growing up I could tell the months by their smell.

First come the fruitstand smells of spring in the city,
Then the backyard trees get back their green, and we know

It's the real thing. Poetry in this puzzle of missing parts
Is best represented by clouds in the early evening sky,

Because they constantly change shape, are utterly indifferent
To us, and seem both remote and near at hand

At once. The creation of the world is a ballet
With the dancers and music missing: what you see

Is a miniature stage-set in a museum display case,
And then suddenly you are walking in it, along the Boulevard Raspail,

Until the Eiffel Tower comes into view. Watch it organize
The bridges of the Seine into a coherent surprise.

XXII.

Love accompanies the stranger to his streetlamp
Encircled by singing insects. The song he hears

Meant doom or wax in the mariners' ears.
And now, as the smell of fresh cut grass gives way to the smell

Of brown leaves burning, I want to tell
You what I heard that night, and how the day

Erased it: I woke to the rattle of a passing car
Which, accelerating up the rapidly rising ramp,

Seemed delighted with its capacity for making noise. From far away
I could hear it coming. And just as we know that fame isn't all

It's cracked up to be, that it can be downright
Nasty in fact, and yet we want it anyway,

So I, too, knew I belonged in one of those cars, tall
Behind the steering wheel, racing to meet the changing light.

XXIII.

Winter came last. Waves of snow from who knows which wind
Turned the meadow beside the frozen waterfall

Into an ocean. The boy in the fairy tale who knew no fear
Soon learned. On the shore of the wide world he could hear

The violins of anger, spelling danger. Poetry in this era of disbelief
Meant staring at a leaf until it turned into a star.

It was easier in the past. All you had to do was sleep outside
And let nature take over. There were more stars in the sky

Than we had room for in our philosophy. And when we woke,
Berries grew beside the burbling brook and bled in our soft hands.

The question was not how like the gods we were
But whether we could recognize them in our sleep

And remember what we had seen, remember them clearly,
When the radio alarm welcomes us into its next musical day.

XXIV.

I live in a boat in front of the door
Depicting the gods as they might have been forgotten

By Lazarus during the tortures of interrogation.
What I see are tombs and yellow stains on the snow.

Instead of quotations, I will refer to my heart;
Instead of an altar, I will guard the munitions

And drink wine with the sour taste of cork
And eat sour strawberries in the city of New York.

You who've been looking for a lost address,
And mothers who seem to be fighting back their tears,

What made you think you could resist the roar
Of the years as they echo in a cavernous subway station?

Can you see the boat in front of the door?
What was it you forgot during the interrogation?

XXV.

Ovid had it wrong. The plight of the frightened maiden
Gliding noiselessly into the woods, like a deer whose eyes

Had been mesmerized by headlights on a cold November night,
Was implausible without the contrivance of arrows: love's dart

Claimed Apollo while the dart of fear pierced Daphne's heart,
And so she ran, deeper and deeper into the woods, losing ground

All the while to Apollo (for love moved faster than fear),
Until the gods, granting her wish, turned the nymph

Into a laurel, which Apollo hopelessly embraced. Poetic justice?
Yes, except it didn't happen that way. Their foot race ended

In a forest clearing, where Daphne, exhausted but unashamed,
Made Apollo watch her undress. He entered her

At her request, as if his will were an extension of her own.
The trees, inclining their branches, nodded in consent. Love won.

XXVI.

The boy, who was more eager than his father
To live on a raft, sleep in the woods, and study the stars,

Became his father, but not before he hid in a cave, slept in it
Overnight, and was saved by a spider from sure destruction.

The king's soldiers, hot on his trail, saw the web stretch unbroken
In the mouth of the cave, and assumed that no one was there.

What is the correct interpretation of the spider's web?
To the soldiers it meant desolation; to the spider, conquest;

To the grandfather telling the tale, providence. The boy
Sees the dew cling to the web at dawn. The natural camouflage

Of rabbits and snakes isn't lost on him. He notices
The triangle formed by three birds in the bare-branched sycamore.

He can hear the hum of a bee admiring a tulip's genitalia.
And at night, he knows, all the colors are present in the white of the
    stars.

XXVII.

That was the year I first read Hölderlin.
The evening fell more slowly and the first day of spring

Arrived more suddenly and stayed lovelier longer.
Boys pursued muses and girls impersonated them.

With the instinct of insects, He and She on the meadow
Mate. What they dreamed stays real when they wake up

In the evening of the first day of spring.
Did they fall out of paradise or were they pushed?

It's unclear, but we next see them enter the gathering dusk,
Hand in hand, and the camera pulls back and the voiceover says,

"Good fortune is even harder to bear
Than the bad fortune that came first. Remember this

About the gods: their own immortality suffices them.
The source of all rivers is a riddle even I cannot solve."

XXVIII.

How little I have changed since then, or how much
Of the change is in the eyes of the beholder

Of a book I lived rather than wrote, whose author
Seems like a stranger to me today. I remember,

For example, wanting to write an apocalyptic parody
Of Milton, in Milton's high style, titled "Eden in Flames."

Adam and Eve celebrated their carnality, and when they woke,
The branches of the fruit trees curved gracefully down

And served them nectar. I couldn't bring myself to describe
Their banishment, and so the project failed. Yet what I heard

When I slept sounded a lot like the chorus of joy
In Beethoven's Ninth, and what I saw when I woke up,

If only for the length of a dream, was a deer,
Eyes mesmerized by headlights, motionless in the middle of the road.

XXIX.

You could be the only passenger on the bus
Who notices that the driver is blind. I, by contrast,

Have eyes only for lovely you. Give me your hand.
I will kiss it. You are cordially invited to my studio,

Which resembles a psychiatrist's office. Once there, I put on my
    glasses,
Read passages out loud from Plato, Hobbes, Marx, and Freud,

And ask you for your opinion of each. Together we analyze
Solitude. There is a meeting of the minds,

And sex follows. It's the first day of spring, and we want
To walk along the river and roll on the grass and take off

Our clothes while leaving the windows wide open. In fact,
We can't wait to get off this bus, which seems to be going

Nowhere fast, as Spring puts her tongue in my ear
And names the forbidden parts of her body.

XXX.

No one could say what the nightmare meant
In the operating theater or the circus tent.

And none of this will help us pay the rent:
Many are called and sleep through the ringing,

But we know it's spring, though we've thrown our watches away.
Our dreams, stretching across the chasm of day,

Don't deter us from waking, jumping into our clothes,
Dancing down the avenue, and swinging through

The revolving doors of the future, where we used to live,
The day before yesterday, when we weren't dying.

—The question is whether the raven will return
After his end-of-the-world adventures, after the storm,

When one by one the masks slip off, and the bride embraces
The guilty son: true to the test, remembered and confessed.

Part Three

The Desire for Strange Cities

1.

Each street means something other than it says.
On Haste Street in Berkeley, the temptation to amble
Down the hill, lazy as a guitar imitating the rain,
Is irresistible, and on Blake Street, a few blocks away,
The cross streets have names like "Jerusalem" and "Thel,"
Or they should. Meanwhile, on 74th Street in Manhattan,
Between Amsterdam and Columbus, it shall always be 1974.

2.

Parlor game: in which city do you imagine yourself
And what do you imagine yourself doing
At the moment when, without warning or apology,
The world comes to an end? Variant: imagine
The circumstances of your own death. Assume,
No doubt erroneously, that death occurs only
When we have readied ourselves for it and that
We do this in our dreams. In the dream you have
All cities and all time zones to choose from.
Where will it be—at an oyster stand near
The intersection of two broad boulevards in Paris,
A London club in 1850 or a Viennese coffee house
Fifty years later? A smoky upstairs bedroom in the Casbah?
Getting off a bus in Jerusalem, at night?

                           I saw myself
In Vienna, where I've never been, walking on a street
Much like the Rue Soufflot in Paris. I swear I saw
Lightning while the sun was out, and it gently rained.

3.

The traveler regaled us with stories, touching and true,
About the people he had met on his sojourns
In strange cities. Better yet were the stories
Edged with menace: the sense that something odd
Was about to happen in the railway station in Milan,
And it did, only his train had long since departed
And he was nearing Geneva when the bomb in Milan
Went off; or the story about the corpulent man,
Bewigged and wearing a judge's black robe
At La Coupole in Paris, over a cafe creme one morning
In 1977, who confided to the table at large
That news of Elvis Presley's death would be
Reported a week later—which happened,
Thus quickening interest in the corpulent man,
Who had disappeared in the meanwhile. But best of all
The traveler's tales were the ones he made up—
No, not made up, recalled—of cities
Where he had never been: sinister Berlin and seedy Sofia,
The carved portals of Vienna in its brilliant light,
Copenhagen during an unseasonably warm December,
Rio, Buenos Aires, Haifa, Hong Kong, Prague.

You don't know who these people are, or what
They'll do to you if you're caught, but you can't
Back out now: it seems you agreed to carry
A briefcase into Germany, and here you are,
Glass in hand, as instructed. You rise to dance
With the woman with the garnet earrings, who is,
Of course, the agent you're supposed to seduce
And betray within the hour. Who would have known
You'd fall in love with her? Elsewhere the day
Is as gray as a newsreel, full of stripes and dots
Of rain, a blurred windshield picture of Pittsburgh,
But on the screen where your real life is happening
It is always 1938, you are always dancing
With the same blonde woman with the bloodshot eyes
Who slips the forged passport into your pocket
And says she knows you've been sent to betray her,
Or else it is seventy degrees and holding
In California, where you see yourself emerge unscathed
From the car crash that wiped out your memory,
Your past, as you walk into a gambler's hangout
On Sunset Boulevard, in a suit one size too large,
And the piano player plays "Perfidia" in your honor
And the redhead at the bar lets you buy her a drink.

Henry James: The Movie

The film begins in Venice
As conceived by the dreamer before
He begins his journey, which ends
At the Bridge of Sighs, where the college friends
Quarrel, make up, declare their vows and divide
The city between them. There is
A moment of terror when the gondola
Enters a tunnel and the foolish younger sister
Yields her heart to the conquering hero
Who ends up with egg on his face because,
Well, because Europe was wise and old
But also decadent and eager to corrupt
Innocent America, ripe for the plucking,
Like the fruit of knowledge, desired, denied.

He spoke with a slight stutter. She answered
By putting her hand on his, a gesture meant
To soften her reproach. She hadn't forgotten
The snow-lipped balconies of Venice—the image,
That is, not the memory, since the image
Preceded the memory and was sacred to her,
A talismanic phrase she used not to cast a spell
But to break one. It failed her here. "You don't
Understand," he said, refusing her hand, as though
He were determined to be misunderstood.
"I feel like the boy who ran away
Hoping to distract his father and mother
And so put an end to their quarrel in low voices,
Their words too cumbersome to comprehend."

And there is the sickening odor of violets
In the hotel rooms of Venice,

Where man, wife, and mistress live in separate rooms,
And each of them knows that in this city of water,
Whose streets reflect the buildings, the sky,
And the interior lives of privileged tourists,
The woman will betray her husband to their son
Swearing him to secrecy, but everyone
But the sculptor himself (whose friends call him "Master")
Knows he's a fraud, and when the old retainer
Arrives, bearing a spurious document on a tray,
The eloping lovers can feel sad without knowing why
While in the room next to theirs sleeps a man
Who has come to Venice to die.

"Oh, how glad I am that she
Whom I wanted so badly to want me
Has rejected me! How pleased I am, too,
That my Fulbright to India fell through!

The job with the big salary and the perks
Went to a toad of my acquaintance, a loathsome jerk
Instead of to me! I deserved it! Yet rather than resent
My fate, I praise it: heaven-sent

It is! For it has given me pain, prophetic pain,
Creative pain that giveth and that taketh away again!
Pain the premonition of death, mother of beauty,
Refinement of all pleasure, relief from duty!

Pain that you swallow and nurture until it grows
Hard like a diamond or blooms like a rose!
Pain that redoubles desire! Pain that sharpens the sense!
Of thee I sing, to thee affirm my allegiance!"

The audience watched in grim anticipation
Which turned into evil fascination
And then a standing ovation, which mesmerized the nation,
As he flew like a moth into the flames of his elation.

If Ezra Pound were alive today
         (and he is)
he'd be teaching
at a small college in the Pacific Northwest
and attending the annual convention
of writing instructors in St. Louis
and railing against tenure,
saying tenure
is a ladder whose rungs slip out
from under the scholar as he climbs
upwards to empty heaven
by the angels abandoned
for tenure killeth the spirit
(with tenure no man becomes master)
Texts are unwritten with tenure,
under the microscope, *sous rature*
it turneth the scholar into a drone
decayeth the pipe in his jacket's breast pocket.
Hamlet was not written with tenure,
nor were written Schubert's lieder
nor Manet's *Olympia* painted with tenure.
No man of genius rises by tenure
Nor woman (I see you smile).
Picasso came not by tenure
nor Charlie Parker;
Came not by tenure Wallace Stevens
Not by tenure Marcel Proust
Nor Turner by tenure
With tenure hath only the mediocre
a sinecure unto death. Unto death, I say!
WITH TENURE

Nature is constipated the sap doesn't flow
With tenure the classroom is empty
          et in academia ego
the ketchup is stuck inside the bottle
the letter goes unanswered the bell doesn't ring.

One Size Fits All: A Critical Essay

Though
Already
Perhaps
However.

On one level,
Among other things,
With
And with.
In a similar vein
To be sure:
Make no mistake.
Nary a trace.

However,
Aside from
With
And with,
Not
And not,
Rather
Manifestly
Indeed.

Which is to say,
In fictional terms,
For reasons that are never made clear,
Not without meaning,
Though (as is far from unusual)
Perhaps too late.

The first thing that must be said is
Perhaps, because
And, not least of all,

Certainly more,
Which is to say
In every other respect
Meanwhile.

But then perhaps
Though
And though
On the whole
Alas.

Moreover
In contrast
And even
Admittedly
Partly because
And partly because
Yet it must be said.

Even more significantly, perhaps
In other words
With
And with,
Whichever way
One thing is clear
Beyond the shadow of a doubt.

1.

The voyeur and the exhibitionist meet
On the sunny side of the street
And fail to recognize each other,
Drenched in daylight. The painter and his model
Become the philosopher and her pupil.
Up all night, they sleep the day away.

Drawn curtains leak in a little light.
In a sentimental mood, the partners
Perform their coyly sexual dance
In windows, which turn into mirrors
At the vanishing point of resemblance.
No one can tell the difference.

Says she, "There's equality in submission."
He agrees. "Or in mutual enslavement."
That must be why they came
To this dark mirror across the airshaft,
Looking for death, finding it at last,
Gambling that they'd survive it,

And they do, hand in hand, marching
Slowing up the aisles and back out into daylight;
Or did desire turn into despair
As the mirror turned into a movie screen
And they watched their bodies merge
At the vanishing point of resemblance?

2.

Our differences unite us. We seek a refuge
For contemplation, having suffered a military

Reversal, and therefore we've come back
To this cave or cathedral or movie house
Where ignorant athletes once clashed by night
And their children bowed down to false gods
And their children's children—bodiless and bereft of
Belief in an afterlife, or the permanence of love—
Sat like strangers in rows watching patterns on a screen,
Wondering what they might mean. Nobody knew.

These were our parents, in Eden and after;
And rubbing our eyes we long to join them
Though it means a retreat from the world
Of ideal forms we learned about in college
Before knowledge meant power—and was ours,
But only because we were powerless
To resist it, or too dumb to know any better.
A bugle breaks the bearable silence.
The late afternoon light looks bright to us,
While out in the clean suburbs, across the land,
The remnants of the nuclear family stand
Ready for sunset, ready to lower the flag.

Spontaneous Generation

Like finding a ninth-grade algebra textbook in the attic
And remembering your panic when you solved
For unknowns in equations for the first time.
You got to be pretty good at it.
It was your best subject in high school.
Today, of course, they probably don't teach it
The same way anymore. Today is your birthday.
You are 39 years old. "When John Keats
Was your age, he was dead for thirteen years," says
The girl in the magazine office. You laugh on cue
And walk out the door, holding your panic in one hand
And the old algebra textbook in the other.
At the base of the hill, you break into a gallop.

The logarithm of the quotient of any two numbers is equal
To the difference between the logarithm of the numerator
And the logarithm of the denominator. Got that?
A man fired a cannon on top of one hill
And a woman on a distant hill used a stop watch
To measure the time between the flash and the roar.
Our goal was an angel dancing on the head of a match:
Facts plus values equaled knowledge divided by time.
Remember, an inch of topsoil will take nature anywhere
From four hundred to a thousand years. One storm
Can wash it away. Pasteur proved "spontaneous
Generation" false—living things do not grow
Out of dead matter. Yet the popularity of ghost
And vampire stories suggests that the imagination
Isn't satisfied with the scientific explanation
Any more than with the class struggle or theory
Of surplus value as a response to an assembly-line life.

Like learning the language
Of the country of your father's birth,
The old country, which he left 39 years ago
And which has since been eradicated,
So that the language survives only among
The scattered tribes of urban North America:
The obsolete idioms, phrases, theorems come back to you,
And the dreams of successful lust after school:
If you could hear the soundtrack of our minds
As they were, a generation ago.

Spontaneous Combustion

Under the mattress was a day-old newspaper rolled into a scroll,
And in the scroll was a small fortune in bank notes.
They all went up in smoke. First the sheets caught fire,
Then the mattress, the newspaper, the money. Finally,
The bed itself began to rise, ascending to the heights
Of a wandering cloud suspended between rival promontories
In the Alps. The bed disappeared into the cloud and then,
And only then, could the lovers be seen
For the first time, in the splendor of their absence,
As if a blaze of light bulbs had outlined their bodies
In the midnight sky, just to the north of the archer.

It was as if the boy had stayed in the big store
After it closed for the night, had hidden in the men's room
When the lights went out and the clerks went home,
And all at once became aware of music in the darkness,
And crept out to witness a masquerade ball of mannequins.
That dancer, there, in the slippers and pearls! He wanted her
And would have her if only . . . if only her body weren't just
A function of the mind that designed her dress and never
Entered the nave of her nudity. And yet . . . and yet the body
Shedding that dress was real, and equipped with the lips
And hair angels lack: the proof lay there beside him
In the bed. A lover of paradox, he turned away
From the big bright cancellations of night
That announced the new day, and let sleep overcome him,
Him and her, in the levitating bed, in the flames.

Pascal's Wager

1.

The thunder altered everything, starting with the shape
Of the sky. It had once been flat. Now, like the earth,
It was round: the concave part of the spoon,

A mirror in which everything was upside down.
The system of mirrors between the sky and the lake
Was a mistake, like music without sound.

The echo lasted into the night and sounded like thunder.
"I have come to give you the key that opens no doors,"
Said the prophet. And the stars turned black in his honor.

2.

The patron saint of lost causes bids me to be religious.
The argument is melodious, seductive.
Religion is based on the revelation that it's over.

Religion and lamentation are one, and therefore
The elegy is the most religious of poetic forms.
Churches attract us as monuments do. In France

We went to Chartres and Amiens and Reims and Rouen,
All the grand cathedrals. They meant more to us
Than the royal gardens or the castles along the Loire.

3.

But at the inevitable zinc bar of a bright cafe
Where Blvd Montparnasse meets Blvd Raspail,
Somebody figured it out. The insurmountable problem

Of religion in the twentieth century was:
How you gonna keep them down on the farm after they've seen
Paree? So, for a time, it survived among us out of habit,

Objects of nostalgic desire: the prayers
You said when you went to bed as a child,
The songs your father taught you, the words.

4.

The repetition of words: there was the poetry of scripture,
The same stories with added emphasis every year:
The story of Joseph, my father's name, the story of my own, David.

Beauty of ritual, discipline, ceremony:
The cup of wine and two loaves of bread on Friday night,
And the double candlesticks glowing in the dark.

There was the sense of being part of a collective destiny,
Hurt by our enemies into history. There was
The morality of the survivor, and the memory of thunder.

5.

Faith, from the beginning, resembled gambling. Every prophet
Is a gambler at heart. In the casino of the imagination,
You would meet the true believers at the roulette wheel

Or green-felt table top, where the dice came up seven.
The jackpot was a group portrait of angels
In heaven, which you admired for its representational exactness

Though you felt in your heart that representation
As an aesthetic principle was dead. In abstract art
Lay the future of an illusion, thirty years ago.

6.

Europe was more innocent, not less, than the United States
When we discovered it. We brought the danger and anger
Of New York sidewalks with us, and the freedom.

On the battlefields of Belgium, religion meant row after row
Of crosses in the thick October twilight. Religion was death
Or somebody else's misfortune. Imperialists of the imagination,

We smuggled Greek statuary—proud, erect, nude—
Into the cathedrals we entered like railway stations,
Suitcases in hand, in Paris and London and Madrid.

7.

The result was predictable. Sex became a species
Of religious worship. We heard the arguments against it,
The injunction against idolatry and so forth,

But couldn't resist the logic of our position.
The athlete and the aesthete were one.
There was even the sense that pornography

On blue summer evenings was religion by other means.
Our favorite cafe had turned into a cave, in the south of France,
Where stalactites of strange and wondrous shapes surrounded us.

8.

Then they put a gun in my hand. They made me
Carry a lit candle as I sleepwalked in the dark.
I walked in my sleep every night for months.

My dreams were listed on the index of forbidden books.
In the darkness I went in my canoe, for you. I sent messages
From "Totem Pole" to "Love Box" with my ham radio

Assembled from parts purchased by answering an ad
In a comic book. My soul was entertained
By the knowledge of its ignorance. Art meant indifference.

9.

Indifference to suffering, except your own: not a very noble
Formula, yet one in widespread use. The poet
Of sensations affirms many things. Pleasure, desire,

Fulfillment, happiness, and joy are the five points
Of his star. Yet in the emptiness of night,
Until our eyes get used to the darkness, the lit candle

Of the sleepwalker is what we need to see by
As we make our way forward, afraid of the dark
Yet more afraid of standing still, wandering in nomad's land.

1.

The two great popular statements
Of the American religion are
(A) Take it easy, and
(B) Don't trust anyone. My father
Went to England in 1953 and said
"Take it easy" instead of "goodbye"
And his sisters in Manchester were
Still talking about it in 1969.
Taking it easy was the American
Way of making money, the face
On the dollar bill that winked
When no one was looking. *In God*
We trust. All others play
The sucker born every minute
In the backseat of the Packard
Where the adulterous liaison began
Between Dolly and the confidence man.
Neither trusts the other
Or blames anyone else. In Cape Cod
People tired of talking about God
Were taking themselves seriously,
Taking it easy after a week on Wall Street,
And the noise was deafening,
The ear too close to the shell,
The lips too close to the microphone,
While in the forests of upstate New York
The American religion was coming into its own.

2.

Remember the time
You asked a curly-haired harp player for a dime
To buy a cup of coffee, and he
Reached in his pocket and took out a cup of coffee?
That was the American religion for you:
Boundless faith, optimism, a hole in my pocket,
And the conviction that language isn't a biological organism
And we aren't its slaves. Emissaries
From the land of pain have come to the land of bread;
I keep calling you back but the phone's busy
Or else I hear the silence of the infinite spaces
Where the students are encouraged to make the connections
On their own, and the bible of each man
Is his alone, no priests necessary, no atheists
In the foxholes or the hospital waiting rooms.
The American religion was the loneliness
Of the deerslayer paddling his canoe
Toward the rapids. It was the man
On the street who couldn't be beat. It was
The boy whose father was dead. The signs
Were interpreted by the analysts
Of our culture, no two of them alike,
Yet their reports were identical, word for word,
With every word erasing the last, and we,
Who had always cherished the idea of a tabula rasa
Knew we could begin again, could begin
Being again, and did.

For I Will Consider Your Dog Molly _____

For it was the first day of Rosh Ha'shanah, New Year's Day, day of
    remembrance, of ancient sacrifices and averted calamities.
For I started the day by eating an apple dipped in honey, as ritual
    required.
For I went to the local synagogue to listen to the ram's horn blown.
For I asked Our Father, Our King, to save us for his sake if not for
    ours, for the sake of his abundant mercies, for the sake of
    his right hand, for the sake of those who went through fire
    and water for the sanctification of his name.
For despite the use of a microphone and other gross violations of
    ceremony, I gave myself up gladly to the synagogue's sensual
    insatiable vast womb.
For what right have I to feel offended?
For I communed with my dead father, and a conspicuous tear rolled
    down my right cheek, and there was loud crying inside me.
For I understood how that tear could become an orb.
For the Hebrew melodies comforted me.
For I lost my voice.
For I met a friend who asked "is this a day of high seriousness" and
    when I said yes he said "it has taken your voice away."
For he was right, for I felt the strong lashes of the wind lashing me by
    the throat.
For I thought there shall come a day that the watchmen upon the hills
    of Ephraim shall cry, Arise and let us go up to Zion unto the Lord
    our God.
For the virgin shall rejoice in the dance, and the young and old in each
    other's arms, and their soul shall be as a watered garden, and
    neither shall they learn war any more.
For God shall lower the price of bread and corn and wine and oil, he
    shall let our cry come up to him.

For it is customary on the first day of Rosh Ha'shanah to cast a stone
into the depths of the sea, to weep and pray to weep no more.
For the stone represents all the sins of the people.
For I asked you and Molly to accompany me to Cascadilla Creek,
there being no ocean nearby.
For we talked about the Psalms of David along the way, and the story
of Hannah, mother of Samuel, who sought the most robust
bard to remedy her barrenness.
For Isaac said "I see the fire and the wood, but where is the lamb for
the offering?"
For as soon as I saw the stone, white flat oblong and heavy, I knew
that it had summoned me.
For I heard the voice locked inside that stone, for I pictured a dry
wilderness in which, with a wave of my staff, I could
command sweet waters to flow forth from that stone.
For I cast the stone into the stream and watched it sink to the bottom
where dozens of smaller stones, all of them black, gathered
around it.
For the waterfall performed the function of the chorus.
For after the moment of solemnity dissolved, you playfully tossed
Molly into the stream.
For you tossed her three times, and three times she swam back for her
life.
For she shook the water off her body, refreshed.
For you removed the leash from her neck and let her roam freely.
For she darted off into the brush and speared a small gray moving
thing in the neck.
For this was the work of an instant.
For we looked and behold! the small gray thing was a rat.
For Molly had killed the rat with a single efficient bite, in
conformance with Jewish law.
For I took the rat and cast him into the stream, and both of us
congratulated Molly.

For now she resumed her noble gait.
For she does not lie awake in the dark and weep for her sins, and
    whine about her condition, and discuss her duty to God.
For I'd as lief pray with your dog Molly as with any man.
For she knows that God is her savior.

Part Four

We who didn't go to Vietnam
Planned our lives around it just the same.
The first thing we said to each other was,
How are *you* going to get out of the army?
It was the year of the lottery:
Each birthday was tagged with a number
And if yours was low enough, you went
For a physical at draft headquarters
Where you saw boys you hadn't seen
Since you were in kindergarten together.
It was the year of the psychiatrist:
I said I was living in despair
And he replied, "Hah! What do *you* know
About despair?" Then we were thrust
Into a locked room, blindfolded,
And after the eye test, when we could see again,
A man in a military uniform
Who might have been a doctor or a priest
Dealt us tarot cards. I drew
The two of cups and the seven of wands.
The doctor went to the sink to wash his hands
And said, "See you in Vietnam."
The priest blessed us. It was the year
Of tear gas dispersing the protesters at Fort Dix,
Students in denim on one side of the fence
Saying, "We're on your side," to the raw
Recruits on the other side of the fence,
Who jeered. We were lucky. We didn't go.
Everyone had a different method for staying out.
Chuck said you could pack peanut butter
Up your ass and then, when you had to drop

Your trousers at draft headquarters,
You reached down and tasted it. It was the year
Robert Kennedy was killed and we
At Columbia went on strike. A bearded boy
Threw a brick through a library window
And called it a critique of pure tolerance.
Herbert Marcuse came to the campus,
As did the Grateful Dead. But even when I read
Plato, I couldn't get my mind off Vietnam.
Some of the guys got their 4-Fs with ease.
Art had track marks on his arm and Stuart
Had been seeing a shrink since he was twelve.
Robbie said he was going to go to Canada,
And did. Some numbers never came up.
We were the lucky ones. The ones who went
Were forgotten. And I am thinking of them today,
Thinking of death in Vietnam, and the dead bodies
That might have been ours, bodies
Tagged and bagged and stacked, before the last
Helicopter lifted off the embassy roof
And the war, *our* war, was over.

Cambridge, 1972

1.

Rob B. came in, chuckling. He had found the quintessential
    Beckett short story.
It began: I was young then, feeling awful.
Then Larry came over with his list of suicidal poets
And everyone decided to write a poem in the form of a suicide
    note.
Mine ended: And that's what they're going to find in my pocket
    tomorrow morning, folks.
It was an imitation of Mayakovsky's last poem but
I don't remember how it began. Charlotte came up
And took off her clothes as soon as Larry and Rob stepped outside
To fight it out over Sandra, who stayed in London awaiting the
    results.
Charlotte's terms of endearment included: my pet, my duck, and my
    chuck.
She was Australian and smoked jasmine cigarettes. Rob B. was
    South African
And kept picking up the girls everyone else fell in love with.
Rob A. was a Californian via Yale who ran a 4:10 mile in high
    school
And borrowed my leather vest which I still have and which I
    should have given him.
We were best friends and when I returned to America he moved in
    with Charlotte
After explaining what Marcuse meant by "reification" and
    "repressive desublimation."
Larry said: "I want to be the poet of Detroit." Then Sandy came
    over with some hash
And made tea and showed us how to win against the Sicilian Defense,
And we all went to the Arts Cinema to see *Wages of Fear*.
When we got there we realized we didn't remember how.

2.

God's name was an audible image at 10 o'clock. At 11 Donatello
    revived the great bronze nude.
At noon we chose among Auden's adjectives. Charlotte voted for
    "clever hopes."
I liked "habit-forming pain." Then we went to the Eagle or the
    Pickerel
And drank a pint of Greene King and ate Scotch Eggs. Alan came
    over and said "what
Do you think of this?" and read us a twenty-page short story
    called "A Girl Named Tweedy."
I said it was a very good title. Then Lew came by fresh from
    Paris in his blue velvet suit
With Becky the piano girl at Fagin's. Lew thought Joan Miró was a
    woman.
The literary magazine came out and it had eleven poems by eleven
    different poets
Each titled "The Old Man." Professor H., introducing Robert
    Lowell
At a poetry reading, called him "one of the greatest living poets"
Adding: "And I think we can safely remove the word living from
    that description."
He meant it as a compliment, but Lowell looked ashen-faced.
At the Round Church, a symposium: Does God Still Wear A Blazer?
Next week: The Vertigo of Relativity. And the week after:
"Imagination is reason in her most exalted mood."

3.

Rob B. wrote a poem called "The Real America," never having been
    there.
Sandy in his Kant phase took a walk down Trinity Street, turned
    into Clare, crossed the Cam
And headed back over the Mathematical Bridge at three sharp every
    day.

His Wittgenstein period came next. Larry said "here's another
    suicidal poet
I think you'll like" and read me the poems of Pavese.
I was in my Groucho Marx period and Lew was in his Frank Zappa
    period
And Charlotte was in her Ginger Rogers period and Larry was in
    his Motown period.
I translated the prose poems of Henri Michaux, my favorite being
    "Simplicity"
In which the poet takes his bed with him whenever he goes outside.
If a woman passes by and catches his eye, why, he takes her to
    bed immediately.

4.

I remember the Brussels sprouts and boiled potatoes, the one
    Cornish hen supposed to feed fifteen
At the house of the Clare chaplain, who visited the rooms of the
    seriously ill.
The dog walked in and peed on the carpet and the chaplain's wife
    said "Oh, Rosebud, you're being boring."
Boring seemed to mean anything but. When the word came up in
    Uncle Vanya
The whole audience burst into laughter. But we all tried to look
    solemn in the chaplain's house.
The food itself looked famished, especially the vegetables.
Rob A. came over and the lights went out because of the coal
    miners' strike.
I was on page 523 of *The Brothers Karamazov* and we talked about
    Dusty (we called him Dusty)
And Nietzsche (who never did betray the heart that loved him).
Then Eve came over, who looked like Ingrid Bergman in
    Notorious,
And Alan came over with his tennis racket
And Hillary came over and complained that Cambridge men were
    impotent

And I wore jeans and a tweed jacket with a fat paisley tie
And Lew married Joyce who became a radical lesbian in Arizona
And Charlotte married a laconic French engineer who wore suits
    from Ted Lapidus
And Rob A. went to Canada and Rob B., back to South Africa,
And Sandy is still smoking his pipe and making Lapsang Souchong
    tea
And Larry is explaining how Sam Cooke was shot to death
As we get into the cab that will take us to the station
Down to London, to Heathrow Airport, to return to the United
    States.

1.

"They're invisible and God is blind," Ron says I said,
And it seemed like the right answer at the time
Though neither of us remembered
What the question was. "Every dead man has one
Phone call coming to him," I'm alleged to have added
The night Ali knocked out Foreman in Zaire
On the radio of some upper Broadway bar
Known only to the two of us, and the inevitable femme fatale
Who sidled up and said, "My monkey's wild," meaning
Whatever. Whatever worked: that was the principle
Behind our cryptic aphorisms, haikus that refused
To be epigrams. Byron played first, Shelley second, and Keats
    shortstop
On my Romantic all-star team, with Billie in the background
And Ron reading Rilke aloud, as we collaborated
On the typewriter in his Eleventh Avenue living room where
It was always three a.m. Godard met Miss America and asked,
"Are drugs a spiritual form of gambling?" I was on an espresso high:
"My heart is thumpin', you started somethin', with them there eyes."

2.

Spend a few hours here and you start talking to yourself,
Like everyone else in the joint. The American idiom
Was a beggar in the bathroom menacing a sophomore with a toy gun:
"Do you got a piece of candy for me? A stick of gum? A cookie?"
If everything is evidence, everything is admissible,
And my tape recorder proves it. I'm thinking of the cabbie
Who turned around, apropos of nothing, and snarled:
"You know what I seen? Blonde girls, blue-eyed beautiful, sucking
    nigger cock *for a dollar*."

He italicized the last three words. I wrote it down, I wrote
Everything down, as though it would otherwise disappear,
As though everything was meant to end up in a book.
And Jamie was sleeping with Amy and I with Beth,
Or maybe it was the other way around.

3.

Auden was asked whether he believed in free love.
"Surely, if it isn't free, it isn't love," he said.
And if it *is* free, it isn't money,
So Ron and I signed on to write filler for a book called *Future Facts*
About the wondrous things the future had in store for us
Like a vaccination against syphilis
And voice detectors to fight crime
And how shit could be recycled into food
For astronauts. I filed away the formula somewhere, or Ron did.
The boss wanted upbeat quotations for the margins. The day I quit
I brought in Orwell: "If you want a picture of the future,
Think of a boot stamping on a human face—forever."
The boss said: "That's not what I want to see in the future."
"But what you want to see and what you will see aren't necessarily
    the same,"
I replied, more interested in a good parting shot than the truth,
Unless fear was the truth and the truth could kill you.
Nana accused me of wearing an affected nonchalance, and I agreed,
    reasoning that
Irony was the best defense against the threat of extinction,
Which I felt daily, for no good reason, and which made sex sexier
In New York, the capital of my mind, in 1974.

4.

I lived with Ed and Josh and Jamie.
Ed had been to Vietnam with the Marines and screamed in his sleep

And told stories about savage drill instructors
And said, about the latest in a long line of lovely skirts,
"I'd dribble a basketball through a minefield for a sip of poison from
   her well."
He was from Virginia and Josh was from California
And memorized Chinese ideograms while watching *Chico and the
   Man*,
Eating peanuts and throwing empty beer cans at the TV
During commercial breaks. Ed held forth over dinner:
"The following individuals should be executed immediately,"
   followed by
A list of politicians celebrities TV anchormen and his own former
   bedmates.
We were drunk. Jamie, all charm, played Bud Powell at the piano
When he wasn't reading *The Naked and the Dead*
And imitating Marlon Brando in *The Godfather*, the greatest
   American film since *Citizen Kane*.
Neither of us knew what he wanted to do with his life.

5.

Nor did anyone else. I took a job ghosting the autobiography of an
   elderly lady
Who turned out to be an amnesiac. Then a graduate student at
   Columbia
Asked me to translate a book of poems from the Greek and when I
   said I didn't know Greek
She said it didn't matter. Recent Barnard graduates and Radcliffe
   graduates, oh,
And French teachers and German teachers and actresses disguised as
   waitresses
And nurses and editorial assistants and dancers who lived on West
   83rd,
Amy Beth Carol Doris Elaine and Fran,
In love with you, with all of you, I am, can't help myself, feeling

Like a dog at the mercy of his tongue, unable to think straight,
And was going to edit a literary magazine called *Young Lust*
But didn't because an impatient finger pressed the up button
Five times in one minute, waiting for the elevator to come
And lift me to her penthouse apartment
Where she twisted her nude body like a discus thrower.

6.

It was she, my nameless blonde asthmatic goddess, who
Told me the story, a Russian fairy tale, about
An old man climbing a beanstalk carrying his old wife
In a burlap bag. As he nears the hole in the sky he'd carved
With his penknife on a previous trip, he slips
And, fighting to regain his balance, drops the bag,
And his wife breaks up into numerous bones,
And we next see him crying on the ground next to the bag of bones.
She didn't say how the story ends, but you can guess. He wanted her
And she wanted him, and from behind the tree an effigy
Of Eve emerged, holding out an apple in her hand. Both
Of them ate greedily. It was the tree of forgiveness.

7.

Somewhere in this city there's a Kafkastrasse
Though you can't tell where it is, mustn't look too hard,
And are bound to get lost on the journey, as we did.
Got to keep going: between the arrow and its target were
An infinite number of detours, and we wanted to take them all,
Take them wherever, as long as we're together, humming along.
Take the A train. Item: drunkard falls on subway tracks,
And the teenage boys who rescue him promptly lift his wallet.
Item: Steve and Rita, moving to San Francisco, parked their packed car
In front of my building and came up for a goodbye cup of Bustelo.
By the time they went back down, twenty minutes later, all their stuff
    was gone,

The windshield smashed, and the vandals had raided the oil tank
To decorate the seats: Ron called it the New York touch.
What I like about this city is
The background music, one hundred percent pre-bop jazz,
The girl on the bus whom you will never see again,
Gray dawn, the fog lifting, the buildings renewing their assault on the
     sky,
The Empire State Building like a giant injection,
And history is being made but like the biography of an amnesiac
It's a different fiction every day, image yoked violently to image,
And literature comes to life: Hamlet crosses the street
And is hit by a car for his impertinence. That was freedom,
A car speeding through a red light at 100th Street and Broadway.
The body covered by a raincoat remained in the gutter
Long after the crowd dispersed, went home, went to work, went to
     sleep.
How did it happen? They were invisible and God was blind.

In the remote country mansion,
A convention of eccentrics was in progress.

In the chapel of crazy voices,
Each of us had to name his favorite tree—
Aleppo pines, umbrella pines,
Mimosa, laurel, the poplars of the paintings,
Palms of Provence—
And the winning portrait was the oval
Shape of a monk's face
Devoid of features: sans eyes, sans nose, sans everything.
That's when you said: "*chasuble* is the most
Beautiful word in the language." Amid such presentiments
Of death as the day provided, the dove wiped
His dirty wings on my shirt, then used
My shoulder for a launching pad
In the sculpture garden outside.

Still life in French means dead nature
But that didn't stop us from arranging our rooms
To fit the requirements of the museum. Still life
With clarinet meant ships in the harbor, an orange moon.
Still life with nude turned out to be a triptych:
In the first panel she wears a wristwatch,
In the second a pearl necklace, in the third fancy glasses:
Somebody's idea of an ad campaign
For the city of Paris. "I need my daily dose of *Le Monde*,"
You said, so we headed to the first cafe
On our list of cafes with great names:
I think it was Le Chat Qui Fume or maybe La Nuit Des Rois.
In walked an American girl wearing a T shirt
On which a bee in a great show of flutter

Says, "I just laid my honey." Cool detachment
Of ten o'clock: red birds, blue skies.

Still life with pears, lemons, and almonds is
A carafe of red wine and three empty glasses
A geranium on a black silk blouse
An oyster shell. That was the day we were going to solve
The problem of esthetics versus ethics
By ignoring the latter as we drank our blond beer,
At Les Bons Enfants or maybe it was Bivouac Napoléon.
(Imagine the New York equivalent: Ike's Trench on Broadway.)
"The point," you said, "is to write everything down."
I began with your habit of saying *and* instead of *or*.
It was I who remembered the pinball machines of desire.
You were too busy playing the violins of anger.

And still are: but if there could be a color to the rain,
An ode to the present that would
Eliminate the need for nostalgia later, who could resist
The climactic cloudburst taking place in our hearts?

"Hence loathed Melancholy! In favor of pleasure we are
And thus have come to the cafes of Europe
Like heroines of Henry James. In our dreams we shall have
A philosophical discussion of the nature of love
And see who can drink whom under the table. We will 'read
Into the general wealth of [our] comfort
All the particular absences of which it was composed'
(James, 'The Great Good Place'). We will buy
Postcards of paintings never looked at, pick berries
On deserted hill tops, lose our luggage
At the vast glass railway station of the future
With the sublime indifference of cats. For never shall there be

A clock in a still life, where eternity is arrested
As tall windows worth leaping out of
Fling themselves open on Mediterranean balconies

To prove that all our nightmares are comic—
A rooster made of ribbons,
A pair of pliers like a calf's skull in profile—
In the cool rooms of the museum
Where the paintings look at the spectators
And smile at the many sizes of the real."

We were smoking some of this knockout weed when
Operation Memory was announced. To his separate bed
Each soldier went, counting backwards from a hundred
With a needle in his arm. And there I was, in the middle
Of a recession, in the middle of a strange city, between jobs
And apartments and wives. Nobody told me the gun was loaded.

We'd been drinking since early afternoon. I was loaded.
The doctor made me recite my name, rank, and serial number when
I woke up, sweating, in my civvies. All my friends had jobs
As professional liars, and most had partners who were good in bed.
What did I have? Just this feeling of always being in the middle
Of things, and the luck of looking younger than fifty.

At dawn I returned to draft headquarters. I was eighteen
And counting backwards. The interviewer asked one loaded
Question after another, such as why I often read the middle
Of novels, ignoring their beginnings and their ends. When
Had I decided to volunteer for intelligence work? "In bed
With a broad," I answered, with locker-room bravado. The truth was,
    jobs
Were scarce, and working on Operation Memory was better than no
    job
At all. Unamused, the judge looked at his watch. It was 1970
By the time he spoke. Recommending clemency, he ordered me to go
    to bed
At noon and practice my disappearing act. Someone must have loaded
The harmless gun on the wall in Act I when
I was asleep. And there I was, without an alibi, in the middle

Of a journey down nameless, snow-covered streets, in the middle
Of a mystery—or a muddle. These were the jobs
That saved men's souls, or so I was told, but when

The orphans assembled for their annual reunion, ten
Years later, on the playing fields of Eton, each unloaded
A kit bag full of troubles, and smiled bravely, and went to bed.

Thanks to Operation Memory, each of us woke up in a different bed
Or coffin, with a different partner beside him, in the middle
Of a war that had never been declared. No one had time to load
His weapon or see to any of the dozen essential jobs
Preceding combat duty. And there I was, dodging bullets, merely one
In a million whose lucky number had come up. When

It happened, I was asleep in bed, and when I woke up,
It was over: I was 38, on the brink of middle age,
A succession of stupid jobs behind me, a loaded gun on my lap.